RAILWAYS OF WALES

Amgueddfa Genedlaethol Cymru
National Museum of Wales

The railways of Wales cannot be portrayed by a single photograph. However, this view of a coal train being assisted by the gradient from Pyle to Stormy Down on 14 March 1962 goes a long way towards fulfilling this requirement. Most of the early railways in Wales were built for the purpose of carrying minerals and this locomotive is one of the 42XX class, specifically constructed by the Great Western Railway for the South Wales coal traffic. (R. O. Tuck)

RAILWAYS OF WALES

By Stuart Owen-Jones
of the
Welsh Industrial and Maritime Museum
(National Museum of Wales)

Amgueddfa Genedlaethol Cymru
National Museum of Wales

Cardiff 1986

© National Museum of Wales

First published 1981
Reprinted 1986

Production: Hywel Gealy Rees
Design: Penknife
Typesetting: Characters
Paper: Huntergloss 150 gsm
Printing: South Western Printers

ISBN: 0 7200 0248 6

Acknowledgements

Although this is a relatively short publication, the author has received willing assistance from a large number of individuals and organisations to whom he is greatly indebted for the provision of material. The sources of these illustrations have been acknowledged as appropriate but the author would also wish to express his gratitude, in particular, to Mr. Eric Mountford and to the members of the Welsh Railways Research Circle for their unfailing help and willingness to assist at all times.

Those readers who require more detailed information than that given in this outline treatment will find the following books, published by David and Charles, of particular relevance:

A Regional History of the Railways of Great Britain
   Vol. 11 North and Mid Wales by P.E. Baughan
   Vol. 12 South Wales by D.S.M. Barrie

Forgotten Railways North and Mid Wales by R. Christiansen
Forgotten Railways South Wales by J. Page

A comprehensive series of monographs on many of the individual railways of Wales is also published by the Oakwood Press.

Note: The changes in recent years to more correct Welsh spellings of a number of place names in Wales (e.g. Llanelly to Llanelli) present difficulties in such an account as this. By and large, we have adhered to the original spellings when referring to the titles of the various railway companies, e.g. the Llanelly Railway & Dock Company.

Front cover:
'Castle Class Locomotive emerging from Severn Tunnel into Wales' by Terence Cuneo. (National Museum of Wales)

In their heyday, the railways of Wales presented an astonishing variety for so small a country. It was a variety of rail operations as great as you could find almost anywhere in the world. There were fast express trains carrying passengers from the London terminals to the ferry ports for Ireland, passengers for whom Wales was but part of a lengthy journey. In contrast, little auto-trains wandered slowly along secluded valleys, trains in which every passenger was known to the guard, who generally knew every passenger's business as well! The contrasts ranged from trains of twelve or more coaches, rolling smoothly along the level lines of the north and south coasts of Wales, to the single coach pushed laboriously by a rack-and-pinion locomotive up the steep slopes of Snowdon; from the heavy coal and iron-ore trucks groaning around the tortuous curves of a South Wales valley, to the lightweight pick-up goods on an Anglesey branch line.

Nowadays, much of the former range and scope of these railway activities are but a memory for the older among us. The changes which have so greatly reduced both tracks and traffic are the result of the changing social and economic patterns of the nation. Only future generations will be able to judge if they were desirable changes. Indeed, improbable as it may now seem, it is possible that future energy requirements may make it expedient to reverse some of these changes. And, because so many of these Welsh railways have vanished, it is easy to forget the circumstances that gave them birth, and the effect they had on the communities which they served.

Communication was, of course, the prime reason for railways, but it is the context of this communication that is now so remote from urban and rural life today. When the railway era really began in Wales, at about 1840, long journeys by stage coach took days rather than hours. Cattle were moved on the hoof and might take weeks to arrive at their place of sale. Roads were rarely metalled; carts and wagons had to cope with deeply-pitted tracks, and the output of iron works and copper mines was, in many cases, still carried in panniers on horse or donkey. Indeed, so difficult was communication that many people would never, in their lifetime, undertake a journey of more than ten miles from the village or community in which they lived.

It was against this age-old background, unchanging through the years in much of Wales, that the railways arrived with startling effect. Within a span of barely twenty years, they transformed communication and transport in the principality. They formed a pattern that determined the industrial development of Wales for the best part of a century.

But in the last twenty years or so, the railway network has rapidly contracted. The location of industry is now largely determined, not by the railway, but by roads and motorways. So the railway concentrates today on a small number of main lines, and the continued existence of the more rural and secondary lines depends not on traffic but on social considerations. These social factors stem from the dominant influence the railway once had in Wales. It is a fragile inheritance. Large elements of it can vanish overnight, thanks to political decisions. Depending on individual viewpoints, this may be economic realism, or social shortsightedness. Certainly, what is called 'the romance of the railway' has, in many ways, disappeared. Local steam trains, complete with passengers, are no longer shunted back to attach a milk wagon, and many a grassgrown valley track no longer echoes to a steam whistle, or even a diesel horn. Where Rhymney Bridge Station once stood, there is a road roundabout, and Duffryn Locomotive Depot has gone to make way for a new housing estate. And the metal ribbons, that once linked far horizons, are gone, it seems, for ever. Today's railway system concentrates on bulk freight and high speed passenger services. It deals now in advanced engineering and technology to a degree inconceivable in past years. Yet, if the present level of interest in, and nostalgia for, the railways is any criterion, then it is clear that much of the former romance and fascination of the railways is still with us.

Making Tracks

The use of the word 'railway' is now generally understood to refer to wheels, with flanges, running on the edge of a rail. A tramroad, therefore, implies flangeless wheels running on a plate rail which carried a vertical flange. Such interpretations have, of course, arisen by custom rather than by definition. (The poet Tennyson, never of a mechanical bent, was convinced that, in his day, trains still ran on tramroads when he wrote: 'Let the great world spin for ever down the ringing grooves of change'.) Adopting this usage, railway construction in Wales began in earnest about 1840. But the history of Welsh railways had its origin half a century earlier with the laying down of extensive tramroad networks in south-east and north-east Wales. These tramroads had two functions: to bring raw material to the works, and then to carry the output, or finished product, away. For the latter, tramroads were usually linked with water transport; canals in the south, and the coast and rivers in the north. In all cases they operated with horses. Many of these tramroads were subsequently converted directly into railways, or the tramroad was abandoned and parts of the route absorbed into a newly-constructed railway. An extreme example is, perhaps, the Burry Port & Gwendraeth Valley Railway which was built along the course of a canal. But this could well have been eclipsed by the proposal of the Marquis of Bute in 1898 to convert the Glamorganshire Canal into a railway. Some of these tramroads owed their origin to discontent with the existing transport system – a cause also responsible for the establishment of some of the railways of South Wales.

The tramroad network developed very rapidly. In South Wales this was due to the opening, between 1790 and 1794, of the principal canals: the Monmouthshire, the Brecon & Abergavenny, the Glamorganshire, the Neath and the Swansea canals. This provided the incentive for the total tramroad mileage to increase from roughly 100 miles at the time, to a total of some 400 miles by the period 1830-40. Amongst the more notable of these early tramroads were the **Oystermouth Railway & Tramroad Company**, which launched the world's first public passenger service in 1807; the **Merthyr Tramroad**, on which the world's first authenticated journey by a steam locomotive took place in 1804; the **Sirhowy Tramroad**, which instituted regular steam haulage in the 1830s; the **Duffryn Llynfi and Porthcawl Tramroad**, frequently forgotten, but responsible for the development of Porthcawl as a port; and the **Rumney Tramroad**, which was a relative latecomer on the scene in 1836 but whose existence was central to the formation of the Brecon & Merthyr Railway some years later. In the west of the coalfield the **Carmarthenshire Railway** of 1802 was actually a tramroad primarily concerned with the movement of coal. In Mid-Wales the **Hay Tramroad** in its rural surroundings was relatively unimportant initially but, later on, formed part of the Midland Railway's route from Hereford to Swansea.

With the opening of regular locomotive-hauled passenger and freight traffic on the Liverpool & Manchester Railway in 1830, and the rapid spread of railways elsewhere in England in the early 1830s, pressures grew among industrialists in

A painting, dated 1821, which shows the tramway leading down to Pillgwenlly in Newport and conveying coal from the Western Valleys of Monmouthshire. (National Museum of Wales)

south-east and north-east Wales for railways which would permit a much faster and more efficient freight operation than the tramroad system. At that stage passengers were of little concern. Indeed, on some of the subsequent South Wales railways that relative state of affairs never did alter much. The first railway to make its mark on the South Wales scene was that of the **Llanelly Railway & Dock Company's** line from Llanelli to Pontarddulais. This opened in 1839 and within a year had been extended to Pantyffynnon. The importance of this railway was very soon overshadowed for, in 1840, the **Taff Vale Railway** was opened from the new West Bute Dock in Cardiff to Abercynon and through to Merthyr nine months later. Sponsored largely by the iron masters of Merthyr, because of the inability of the Glamorganshire Canal to cope with the traffic being offered, it was engineered by Isambard Kingdom Brunel (1806-1859), the great Victorian engineer, and architect of the Great Western Railway's broad gauge at 7'0¼". The railway was of single-track throughout. Brunel had recommended the adoption of the standard 4'8½" gauge for the railway because of the sinuous and narrow nature of much of the Taff Valley, but the consequences of this decision were not to become apparent for another twenty years. Traffic on the railway developed rapidly and between 1845 and 1861 the line was doubled throughout. The opportunity was then taken to open out a tunnel between Quaker's Yard and Abercynon and, on the same section, to realign a very short but steep cable-worked incline which had proved to be an operating inconvenience.

Following the partial opening of the Taff Vale in 1840 it is, superficially, rather surprising to find that the next opening of any consequence was ten years later, when the first part of the **South Wales Railway** was completed in 1850. This, however, is a misleading conclusion. There was already in existence in Monmouthshire a far more extensive network of long distance tramways than there was in Glamorgan. This network was primarily intended to carry iron and coal down to Newport and, because of the geography around Newport, there were, realistically, only two routes into the

An 1865 engraving of Blaen-y-Cwm Viaduct, Tredegar, with the Trefil Tramroad in the foreground
(National Museum of Wales)

town from the hinterland. One passed through the River Ebbw gap to the west of the town and the other through the River Usk gap on the eastern side. The longest mileage was operated by the **Monmouthshire Railway & Canal Company** (although this was not its early name) and, while it had a large network around Ponypool, of concern here is the company's tramroad of 1805 from Newport up the side of the Ebbw to Nine Mile Point in the Sirhowy valley. Here it made an end-on junction with the Sirhowy Tramroad which continued on to the top of the valley.

In 1826 the **Rumney Tramroad** ran down from the Rhymney Ironworks and joined the Monmouthshire Company's tramroad near Bassaleg. This tramroad system, however basic, and only partially steam locomotive hauled in the 1840s, still proved capable of carrying a remarkable tonnage of iron and coal down to Newport, despite the inconvenience of running on plate-rails. In the late 1830s and early 1840s, therefore, there was not the pressure to construct a railway that there was in Merthyr. By the late 1840s, however, it was becoming evident to the managements of the three tramroad companies precisely what was being achieved on the Taff Vale railway with its locomotive-hauled trains running on edge-rails. Even in the first year of its operation the Taff Vale had made a profit of over £17,000. Slowly, but inevitably, therefore, the decision was reached to convert their tramroads into railways. This conversion resulted in the finances of all three companies being placed under considerable strain and ultimately in their absorption or takeover. The Monmouthshire Company started its conversion in the 1850s but took nearly a decade to complete it. As a consequence its finances suffered, despite its near monopoly, and in 1875 it was taken over by the **Great Western Railway**. The Sirhowy Tramroad had actually completed its conversion by 1855 and then endured a similar fate later. In this case, however, it was taken over in 1876 by the **London and North Western Railway** which thereby achieved two ambitions – access to a mining valley and access to a port on the Bristol Channel. The Great Western Railway had already largely achieved these ambitions by the time of its takeover in 1876. The Rumney Tramroad started its conversion in 1861 but rapidly succumbed to a bid from the infant **Brecon & Merthyr Railway** and sold out in 1863. In this way the predominant pattern of railway operations in the western valleys was set until the grouping in 1923. (The Railway Grouping of 1923 resulted in nearly all British railways being grouped into four major companies: the L.M.S., the L.N.E.R., the G.W.R. and the S.R.).

The Monmouthshire Company had also constructed a brand-new railway in 1852 to link up with the eastern valleys by means of a line from Newport through Cwmbran to Pontypool, where it met an extensive tramroad network extending further up the valleys. In the following year the **Newport, Abergavenny & Hereford Railway** opened from Pontypool to Hereford and, one year later, a connection was made between this and the Monmouthshire Company's line at Pontypool. This enabled through-running to take place between Newport and Hereford and thence to the developing railway network in England.

One might well wonder at this stage what other railways had been opened in the rest of Wales by the end of the 1840's. This question can be simply answered because in mid and west Wales there was nothing other than the Llanelly Railway,

to which reference has already been made. In North Wales there was one major development, the **Chester & Holyhead Railway**, to be considered shortly. Apart from this, the picture is a sparse one, the sole innovation being the **North Wales Mineral Railway** which opened in 1846. As its name implies, this railway's primary purpose was the carriage of minerals, and it ran from Wrexham to Saltney on the Dee. Before this there had been great difficulty in transporting the products of the rich mineral area around Wrexham, coal, iron, stone and non-ferrous ores, because, although there were a number of tramroads, they had not been developed to the extent of their counterparts in South Wales. This Mineral Railway was rapidly extended to Ruabon and, ostensibly under the guise of an independent company, the **Shrewsbury, Oswestry & Chester Junction Railway**, to Shrewsbury in 1848. The two companies had by now been formally amalgamated into the **Shrewsbury & Chester Railway** and, unlike many other railways which did not go near the towns in their title, this one did actually reach Chester by running over a short length of the Chester & Holyhead Railway at its northern end. Because the line impinged on the rugged terrain of Denbighshire it was expensive to construct but, in the process, it provided two magnificent viaducts to cross the Dee and Ceiriog valleys. The extremities of this railway lie strictly outside the scope of this account, but it is worth noting that the line had a definite strategic importance. The London & North Western Railway had now reached Chester, while the Great Western Railway had access to Shrewsbury. Consequently, whichever company could acquire the intervening link would benefit considerably from the mineral traffic being generated in the Wrexham and Ruabon areas. Despite adopting means which are incredible by today's standards, but not, possibly, by those of an era which could produce the Railway King, George Hudson, with all his machinations, the North Western, nevertheless, lost both the battle and the war. Much to its annoyance, it never subsequently succeeded in penetrating the industrial area around Wrexham.

The Routes to Ireland

Thus far, all the railways we have described were designed mainly for carrying freight and, because they were comparatively short lines, they were built relatively quickly after the date of their incorporation. But there were two other railways, which ran along the north and south coasts of Wales respectively, and whose sole purpose was to use this new mode of transport to make the journey between England and Ireland shorter and safer for people, freight and mail. Carrying mail was especially desirable. It was normally done under long term contract, and so it provided a regular and steady income. Once the successful outcome of the Liverpool & Manchester Railway, opened in 1830, became apparent, the government realised the great potential of railways for improving communication with Ireland. In political and economic terms this was highly significant. The government regarded it as expedient to offer financial encouragement and support for suitable rail proposals. To take advantage of this governmental favour, Charles Vignoles, an ex-army officer, had, by 1836, already surveyed two possible routes. One crossed the northern coast from Chester through Bangor to Holyhead; the other ran more diagonally across Wales to end at Porth Dinllaen. In that same year, 1836, another group of entrepreneurs were discussing a possible line across South Wales, from Gloucester to New Quay in Cardiganshire, with little regard for the potential of coal traffic. This was not, perhaps, lack of foresight; the deep seams of coal in the Rhondda were not to be discovered for several years.

Because the carriage of mail by rail was so much faster and more reliable than by sailing packet it was clearly desirable for the rail portion of the route between London and Ireland to be as long as possible. Thus there was a clear advantage in having the North Wales terminal at Holyhead rather than at Porth Dinllaen, quite apart from the much more favourable terrain. Such a proposal was made by the **Chester & Crewe Railway**, with the support of that 'father of railways', George Stephenson (1781-1848), the erstwhile pit-boy who

Bridgend Station on the broad-gauge South Wales Railway soon after it was opened in 1850. It will be seen that the rails are carried on longitudinal timber baulks.

rose to become builder of the Stockton and Darlington, and the Liverpool and Manchester railways. But Stephenson, self-taught and working by rule-of-thumb and from personal experience, was not acceptable to everybody. His empirical approach led him into many problems which his much more educated son, Robert (1803-1859) would have avoided. The outcome, in 1840, was government agreement on the Chester – Holyhead route, but a further four years went by before the authorising Bill was passed.

Meanwhile, Brunel had re-surveyed a route from Worcester to Porth Dinllaen which, of course, had strengthened the hand of the Chester & Holyhead. Brunel's backing by the Great Western Railway meant that his line would have been a broad-gauge one, and so would have extended the broad-gauge territory. But major problems already raised by the break of gauge in England had resulted in the Gauge Commissioners' report of 1846 recommending that no increase in its territory should be permitted. Thus the Great Western Railway's ambitions in North Wales were temporarily blocked. This adverse report had been anticipated, however, and in 1845 a Bill was passed, with the support of the Great Western Railway, authorising the **South Wales Railway** to

'Victor Emanuel', one of the broad-gauge locomotives operated by the G.W.R. which provided all the locomotives and rolling stock for the South Wales Railway.

Pentyrch Station on the Taff Vale Railway was an early casualty of railway economics, closing in 1863.
(South Glamorgan Library)

be constructed; naturally, to the broad gauge. This support was based on a terminus at Fishguard since the Great Western was still thinking of the Irish traffic and government encouragement, and disregarding the potential iron and coal traffic. The other end of the South Wales Railway was to be at Grange Court where it would meet another line to Gloucester.

There were now two authorised routes to Ireland crossing Wales and construction proceeded apace on both of them. Perhaps it was no mere coincidence that the two greatest engineers of the day, Robert Stephenson and Isambard Kingdom Brunel, acted for the Chester & Holyhead and South Wales Railways respectively. They were, naturally enough, in competition with each other. But they were also good friends. When the enormous task of raising the tubes of the Britannia Bridge was being planned Brunel readily acted as consultant to Stephenson. There is also another incidental link with the past. When Richard Trevithick, who built the Penydarren Locomotive, was in South America and had fallen on hard times he met Robert Stephenson, who helped him financially and at least temporarily relieved Trevithick's difficulties.

Both lines were built across relatively easy terrain but, nevertheless, they presented challenging obstacles to both engineers. On the Chester to Holyhead route, the outstanding feature was, of course, the crossing of the Menai Straits by the Britannia Bridge. This used the then revolutionary principle of carrying the trains through wrought iron tubes. Because this kind of structure was so new, and untried, the bridge at Conway was built first as a scaled-down version of the Britannia, in order to get the relevant experience of such a work. Apart from these two bridges there were few other constructional features of note on the line other than a number of tunnels on the Conway – Bangor section. Because of its proximity to the sea over a number of stretches the line has always been liable to damage from storms and erosion and, over the years, there have been some quite spectacular instances of such damage. Apart from a very short length from Saltney to

A Fairlie 0-4-4-0 locomotive of the Neath and Brecon Railway which opened throughout in 1867. (Illustrated London News)

Chester, which was opened in 1846 in conjunction with the North Wales Mineral Railway, the line from Chester to Bangor and across Anglesey was opened in 1848, leaving passengers to cross the Menai Straits by Telford's road bridge until the Britannia Bridge was completed, and thus the line throughout, in 1850. In terms of human endeavour there were, at the peak of construction of the line, some 12,000 men involved, the organisation and management of whom represented a task at least equal to that of any general commanding an army. While the analogy should not be carried too far, it should also be noted that nineteen men alone lost their lives in the construction of the Britannia Bridge. In financial terms construction of the line, and particularly of the Britannia Bridge, exceeded

the estimates and left the railway to pay considerable interest charges once it had opened. From its inception the line was worked by the London & North Western and, despite traffic being reasonably well up to expectations, the railway's finances never prospered. In what might be described as an inspired piece of political manoeuvring the company had discussions with, amongst others, the Great Western Railway. Not surprisingly the North Western rose to the bait and duly acquired the line in 1859. Once the Chester & Holyhead's Bill had received Royal Assent the construction of the line had proceeded reasonably smoothly with the intended destination being reached as Parliament had intended.

Fortune did not smile on the South Wales

FFORDD HAIARN Y GREAT WESTERN.

AT YRWYR A PHERCHENOGION CERBYDAU TRYMION NEU Y PERSONAU SYDD YN GOFALU AM DANYNT.

YN OL Y DDEDDF A BASIWYD YN Y FLWYDDYN 1861, RHODDIR RHYBUDD DRWY HYN NAD YW Y BONT HON YN DDIGON CREF I DDAL MWY O BWYSAU NAG A DDELIR YN NGHYLCH MASNACH GYFFREDIN YR ARDAL HON; HEFYD NAD YW Y PERCHENOG NA'R GYRWR NEU UNRHYW BERSON ARALL Y BYDDO GOFAL Y CERBYDAU ARNO I GEISIO GYRU DROS Y BONT HON HEB GAEL CANIATÂD GAN AWDURDODAU FFORDD HAIARN Y GREAT WESTERN.

TRWY ORCHYMYN.

An early and unusual bridge notice from Bala for which a translation of the title reads 'The Great Western Iron Road'. The 'Iron Horse' was still a meaningful description at that time. (M.E.M. Lloyd)

Railway in quite the same benevolent manner, for its construction started slightly, but significantly, later than the Chester & Holyhead. During this short period the increasing cost of construction and a deterioration in conditions in Ireland and on the economic front generally, caused the South Wales Railway to modify its intentions. It abandoned Fishguard as its destination and diverted its shortened line to Neyland in Milford Haven, a suggestion with which the Great Western Railway, having leased the line, to its annoyance ultimately had to agree. The principal section of the line from Chepstow to Swansea opened in 1850, but the extensions to Carmarthen and to Neyland did not take place until 1852 and 1856 respectively. The northern route to Ireland thus opened six years before the amended southern route. By prior arrangement it was agreed that, once through working between London and Swansea was possible, the Great Western Railway would lease the line and, with the opening of the Chepstow Bridge in 1852, this company duly operated the line, providing all the locomotives and rolling stock.

The line was largely level, but there were four major river crossings. From west to east, they were the Towy Bridge below Carmarthen town, the long, high viaduct across the Tawe at Landore, a bridge over the Usk at Newport (which distinguished itself by going up in flames before the line had opened), and, the biggest challenge, the crossing of the Wye at Chepstow. Brunel's solution here was to carry trains on girders suspended from elliptical iron tubes. As with Stephenson's Conway Bridge, this was also an innovatory design, a forerunner, this time, of the much larger Royal Albert Bridge at Saltash, in 1859.

The parallel with the Chester & Holyhead Railway does not end here. The South Wales Railway's finances also did not fulfil expectations, but for a far more specific reason. With the backing of the Great Western Railway, the line, as has been noted, was inevitably constructed to the broad-gauge. As such it made connection with only one broad-gauge line of significance in South Wales – the **Vale of Neath**. This was also engineered by Brunel and opened from Neath to Aberdare in 1851. As in other peripheral parts of the Great Western Railway, traders disliked the break of gauge from standard to broad and vice versa, especially when South Wales coal was involved because of its friable nature. They preferred to stick to one gauge only, in this case the standard one, and as time passed the addition of two more standard-gauge lines, which tapped the coalfield in 1858, provided them with further alternatives to using the broad-gauge. Thus although the South Wales Railway was not quite ostracised by the coal traders it was certainly unpopular with them. Accordingly the pressure on the South Wales Railway to change to standard-gauge grew inexorably. Under these pressures, financial problems and other disagreements, the South Wales Railway bowed to the inevitable and amalgamated with the Great Western Railway in 1863. Conversion of the broad-gauge line to standard-gauge was now an undisputed necessity and the actual conversion of the entire route took place within the space of a remarkable three weeks in 1872. The final parallel between the railways across North and South Wales is now drawn, with each being taken over by one of the railway giants within eleven and thirteen years respectively of their birth and with their individual identities being submerged forever.

The Coal and Iron Trade

The two standard-gauge lines referred to in the previous paragraph were both of great strategic value for the coal trade. The first was the **Newport, Abergavenny & Hereford Railway's Taff Vale Extension**. This ran due west from Pontypool to a connection with the Taff Vale at Quaker's Yard in 1858. It was a route which crossed, and connected with, nearly all the lines in the intervening valleys, and so provided a lucrative source of mineral traffic. Because it crossed these valleys, its construction involved masive earthworks and numerous bridges. The largest, and certainly one of the most impressive in Britain, was the Crumlin Viaduct, which was in continuous use for 107 years until its demolition in 1965. This was an elegant iron lattice-work structure which reduced the effects of wind-resistance in the narrow width of the valley. Even at the time its magnitude was widely appreciated, and the *Illustrated London News* featured its building in several issues.

After another change of ownership the whole of the Newport, Abergavenny & Hereford line, and its extension, passed into the hands of the Great Western in 1863. Within a year the G.W.R. had also acquired the Vale of Neath Railway, which by this time had been converted to standard-gauge and linked to the Taff Vale Extension. So, the Great Western now had a standard-gauge line cutting right across the coalfield and, having taken over the South Wales Railway, could feel well satisfied with its policy of territorial aggrandisement.

The second line in question was the **Merthyr, Tredegar & Abergavenny Railway**, whose avowed intent was to connect the first and last towns of its name by a line which, after an initial climb, ran across the heads of the valleys. In theory it could throw off branches to each of the valleys in turn, and so offer the coal-owners and ironmasters a far more convenient route to the rapidly growing manufacturing areas of the Midlands. It was an attractive theory, but the construction involved massive earthworks and a severe climb up the precipitous sides of the Clydach Gorge. So heavy

A typical railway prospectus to which many an unsuspecting investor might have been tempted to subscribe at the time of the railway mania in 1865-6. (National Library of Wales)

were the construction costs that the company had to enter into an agreement with the London & North Western Railway even before the first section, from Abergavenny to Brynmawr, was opened in 1862. It is still possible to see much of the track-bed of this line, with its associated brick and stone structures where it climbs up the gorge, and one can imagine the effort involved in hauling a train up an average gradient of 1 in 40 for some eight miles. It is hard to imagine any land reclamation or development scheme which will, in

*A painting of the Taff Engineering Works, Treherbert, dated 1884, with
the Taff Vale Railway in the foreground.
(John M. Gibbs)*

and so continued to the centre of Cardiff. Here the
Rhymney had a branch of its own to the East
Dock. Traffic started in earnest in 1858. Now, all
through the history of the South Wales companies,
which had shared lines and competing traffic, there
was usually trouble sooner or later. The shared line
between Taff's Well and Cardiff was a case in
point. The Rhymney Railway could see little future
in this shared arrangement. Within six years of
opening, the company successfully promoted a Bill
for a direct line from Caerphilly to Cardiff Docks
through the Cefn On tunnel. Construction rapidly
followed and, after a short period of uncertainty,
the Rhymney went from strength to strength; it
gave as good as it got in the various disputes in
which it was embroiled from time to time. This
strength it frequently derived from a phenomenal
man named Cornelius Lundie. He joined the
company in 1862 as engineer and traffic manager,
capacities which today would be regarded as
mutually incompatible, but which he combined in
a remarkable manner. He retained his energies and
his faculties to the last. He died in 1904, at the age
of 93, still contributing to the success of the
Rhymney Railway!

Probably the Rhymney's outstanding dispute
was with the second company referred to earlier,
the **Brecon & Merthyr Railway**. As we have said,
this company had taken over the old Rumney
Tramroad in 1863, when the latter was converting
from tramroad to railway. The Brecon & Merthyr
had actually started life a little earlier with the
express purpose of connecting Brecon to a port on
the Bristol Channel, and the section from Brecon to
Dowlais was authorised in 1859-60. During
construction the company examined various ways
to reach the coast and, fortuitously, the financial
troubles of the Rumney Tramroad readily allowed
it to acquire that route. The only difficulty was the
link between Bargoed and Dowlais. This gave rise
to an exceedingly acrimonious dispute with the
Rhymney Railway, which also had designs on the
same route. Compromise was the only feasible
solution and so, with a partially shared main line,
the Brecon & Merthyr led a very shaky financial
existence until the 1923 grouping.

the future, obliterate this monument to a
pioneering venture. From Brynmawr the line levels
off considerably, but it still took until 1873 for the
L.N.W.R. to reach Dowlais, above Merthyr. But
by means of the various valley connections, the
London & North Western succeeded admirably not
only in infiltrating the coalfield but also in
obtaining invaluable running powers to Newport,
Cardiff and Swansea.

To complete the picture of railway
development in this part of Wales during 1850-65,
two further companies must be considered. At the
beginning of this period, in the Rhymney and
Sirhowy valleys, iron industry traffic still exceeded
that from coal mines. The Bute Trustees, who
owned extensive ironworks at Rhymney, and who
had opened Cardiff's West Bute Dock and were
planning the East Dock, saw a definite potential in
a new railway from Rhymney to Cardiff.
Supported by nearly all interested parties,
including the Taff Vale, the rapid outcome was the
proposed **Rhymney Railway**. The ready support of
the Taff Vale was due to the final plan, in which
the new line ran from Rhymney to Caerphilly,
thence to Taff's Well, where it joined the Taff Vale,

The Brecon & Merthyr line was one of contrasts. The section from Dowlais, and later Merthyr, down to Newport, was a profitable one. In contrast, the line from Dowlais over the Brecknock Beacons, down to Talybont, and so to Brecon, was a beautiful panorama, but an operational nightmare. This section carried a fair amount of traffic, but it was very little indeed compared with the lower sections and, with its heavy maintenance costs, proved a millstone round the company's neck.

With the completion of these, and the other lines described earlier, the railway network in the eastern half of the South Wales coalfield was now established. It was to remain so for the next twenty-five years. There were, of course, numerous additional lines, connections and spurs to cope with the ever-increasing coal trade. Ultimately, even these failed to satisfy the demands of the coal-owners for more efficient transport of their coal, and for improved loading facilities at the ports. The almost inevitable outcome of this pressure was a demand for a new railway. But this part of the story is premature.

The G.W.R. Station at Wrexham, c.1880. (British Rail)

Into 'Wild Wales'

From our story so far, it will be clear that to treat the railway history of Wales in a completely chronological order would prove, not merely difficult but, more probably, incomprehensible. This is the result of the very rapid expansion of the network in the 1850s and, even more so, in the 1860s. After these two decades, construction quickly tailed off as nearly all the towns, villages and industrial areas with traffic potential were rail-connected. In the aftermath of the second 'railway mania' of 1865-6, there was also a much greater reluctance by investors to subscribe the necessary capital. We can see how concentrated in time this expansion was by measuring the total route mileage of standard gauge lines and major extensions opened in each decade.

Years:	Total route mileage
1830-39	32
1840-49	216
1850-59	285
1860-69	680
1870-79	140
1880-89	136
1890-99	100
1900-09	84

This simple measurement demonstrates how rapidly the expansion occurred. Because of this the purely chronological approach is undesirable. It is more appropriate to consider next the two lines, or systems of lines, spread across the Welsh heartland, which essentially completed the major Welsh network up to the end of the 1860s. These are the so-called Central Wales line, initially a series of contiguous companies, and the group of lines which eventually formed the Cambrian Railways.

The Cental Wales line had a very early beginning in the Llanelly Railway Company's line to Pontarddulais in 1839, but it was another eighteen years before the line reached Llandeilo. A year later, in 1858, the line had been extended to Llandovery. Having started as a purely local concern, its 30 mile length, as viewed from faraway Euston, began to look like an incipient trunk line. This gleam in the London & North Western eye

was due to the intense concentration of metal industries in Swansea, the beginnings of tin-plate making in the Swansea-Llanelli area, and the fact that a possible extension of the line would pass through Shrewsbury (already a major railway centre). To the local industrialists, the idea was also attractive. This would be a standard-gauge line to the North, without the inconvenient and expensive change-of-gauge problems posed by the South Wales Railway at that time. Fortuitously, another local line, from Craven Arms to Knighton, was being planned, which would provide an essential link at the top end of this conjectured Swansea to Shrewsbury route. The gleam in Euston's eye grew brighter and, by 1868, through a series of nominally independent companies, the upper end of the link had been extended down to Llandovery. In that same year, all were absorbed forthwith into the London & North Western!

In 1867, the Llanelly Railway had completed the Pontarddulais-Swansea line. This was a most desirable property for the London & North Western. Five years later, the Llanelly Railway had disappeared; the Great Western and the North Western shared the spoils, and the latter gained greatly from the deal. This railway giant promoted the Central Wales line strongly for both freight and passenger traffic. The spa towns of Mid-Wales were most popular at the time, and gave rise to much long distance and profitable traffic, with through coaches to many parts of England. From contemporary accounts, the arrival and departure of the gentry at Llandrindod Wells station must have compared with the busy scenes at King's Cross when the grouse season opened! But today, with changing social patterns, this traffic has vanished, and the line is now used more for local than through journeys.

The remaining major line was the **Cambrian Railways**, the only Welsh railway to consist of a real network of lines, rather than simply an expanded mineral line. The Cambrian did not begin as a planned major network; it was the result of a pragmatic view taken, by the individual component companies, of the very limited potential for traffic in Mid-Wales. The first component, the

Express train near Wrexham. (Clwyd Record Office)

An early industrial locomotive, 'Henrietta', with coal wagons at the Minera Lead Mine, c.1890. (Clwyd Record Office)

Llanidloes & Newtown Railway, received royal assent in 1853 and finally opened in 1859. There it stood, or rather lay, in splendid isolation in the middle of Wales. Some people did see it as part of a line, but not of a network, which might one day connect Manchester to Milford Haven. But the next stage to be opened throughout was the **Oswestry & Newtown Railway** in 1861. Its backers were mainly local people and organisations. The contractor for both these lines was Thomas Savin, closely associated with David Davies of Llandinam (1818 – 1890), whose perseverance in the Rhondda Valley had finally brought success, and who was reaping the fruits as owner of the Ocean Coal Company. Davies, industrialist, coal-owner and promoter of at least seven lines in Mid-Wales, is best remembered as the 'father' of the Barry Docks & Railway Company. The concept of a relatively large network had now gained in credibility and confidence. Plans were in hand for a line from Newtown to Machynlleth. This was completed in 1862, and two years later had been extended to Aberystwyth. Meanwhile, the **Aberystwyth & Welsh Coast Railway** was building, with a line running north up the coast with Pwllheli as its objective. Completion of the Machynlleth –

Aberystwyth line was thus crucial, because it would allow through traffic from Aberystwyth to Welshpool, and thence to the main lines across the English border. It would also provide an alternative route to the South Wales Railway for destinations south of Aberystwyth.

The year 1864 also saw the amalgamation of the three companies on the Oswestry – Machynlleth route, and the **Oswestry, Ellesmere & Whitchurch Company** to form the Cambrian Railways Company. A year later they were joined by the Aberystwyth & Welsh Coast Company. This line proved troublesome and expensive to construct and it was finally completed in 1867. Completion did not mean the end of the line's troubles, for it suffered many washouts of bridges and track over the years. The misfortunes of the line reached their climax in 1933 when, for the second time on the Friog cliffs (the first being in 1883), a train was derailed by a landslide and fell on to the rocks below. In the early 1860s a modest line known as the **Mid-Wales Railway** had been proposed to run south from Llanidloes to Brecon. It duly reached Brecon in 1864, although for the last few miles from Talyllyn Junction the trains ran over the rails of the Brecon and Merthyr Railway, which had reached Brecon the year before. By analogy with

Some railway company seals were simple monograms while others were pictorial representations of the company's activities. The Lampeter company's seal was a little too ambitious, however, since it never owned any locomotives let alone one of the tender type depicted here. (National Railway Museum)

A Port Talbot Railway freight train near Llangeinor soon after the line opened in 1898. (National Library of Wales)

The Alexandra (Newport) Dock and Railway acquired three coaches from the Barnum and Bailey Circus, two of which were used for the auto-train service between Pontypridd and Caerphilly. (National Museum of Wales)

The G.W.R. and G.C.R. staff at Wrexham Exchange Station. (Clwyd Record Office)

what occurred in other parts of the country, the Mid-Wales Railway should rapidly have been absorbed into the Cambrian Railways. Instead, it eked out an independent existence until 1888 when it reached a working agreement with the Cambrian Railways. It was not finally absorbed until 1904.

While dealing with railway activities in Mid-Wales, reference must be made to a railway which, in relation to its length and the traffic which it carried, has generated more interest, and had more written about it, than possibly any other railway. From the mid-1840s there had been a succession, indeed almost a stream, of proposals for a railway to connect Manchester with Milford Haven, the attraction being to lessen the dependence of the industries of Manchester on the Port of Liverpool and on the monopoly held by the Liverpool & Manchester Railway. Unlike the very prosaic titles of some rail companies such as the Rhymney or the Taff Vale, some of the Mid-Wales proposals at this time had extraordinarily grandiose titles, such as the **Grand North & South Wales Railway** and the **Radnorshire, Aberystwyth & Welsh Midland Junction Railway**, which would have left Aberystwyth and climbed straight inland on a gradient of 1 in 50 for 10 miles!

The **Manchester & Milford Railway**, after numerous plans and even more variations of route, was finally authorised in 1860. The proposed line left the **Carmarthen & Cardigan Railway** at Pencader and ran through Devil's Bridge to Llanidloes where it joined the Llanidloes & Newtown and Mid-Wales railways. The ownership and operation of this junction produced great argument, but the track was duly laid from the junction to Llangurig, some five miles away. During construction, however, the magnitude of the work, and the cost involved, of crossing the mountains near Devil's Bridge became obvious. This, and the manoeuvres of other railway companies, caused a change of mind. The line was diverted at Ystrad Meurig towards Aberystwyth, which was reached in 1867, and the stretch from Ystrad Meurig to Llanidloes was abandoned.

The succeeding fortunes, which were few, and the misfortunes, which were many, of the

Tal-y-Sarn Station with a L.N.W.R. train from Bangor. In front of the train are the horse-drawn wagons of the Nantlle Railway which was also owned by the L.N.W.R. and so duly passed into British Railways' ownership when nationalisation took place. (National Library of Wales)

The Plynlimon and Hafan Tramway had a short life and the passenger service an even shorter one for it only operated in 1898. (National Library of Wales)

A Midland Railway goods train at Devynock in 1903. (T. Watkins)

The Cambrian Railways Goods Yard at Wrexham. (H. Morgan)

Manchester & Milford Railway (whose end result after years of trials and tribulations produced only a 41 mile-long line from Pencader to Aberystwyth) could, and indeed recently have, justified a book all to themselves. It was not a speedy service. In 1872, a mixed freight and passenger train from Pencader to Aberystwyth took 4½ hours, at less than ten miles an hour! Notwithstanding its misfortunes, the company usually retained a sense of optimism and, when the line was only partially open from Pencader to Lampeter, advertised a through journey from Manchester to Milford. But, as R. W. Kidner has so delightfully pointed out, such a return journey would have taken at least a week to complete!

A further example of the extraordinary rapidity with which railway construction proceeded in the period 1860 – 70 is provided by considering Central and North Wales in 1858. In that year there were no railways between the Chester & Holyhead line running along the North Wales coast, with a short line from Rhyl to Denbigh, and, far to the south, the rail and tramroad network across the heads of the valleys in South Wales, and the end of the Llanelly Railway at Llandovery. This rustic remoteness was to be changed in the space of ten years.

As has already been seen, starting with the Llanidloes & Newtown in 1859, virtually the whole of the ultimate Cambrian Railways system had been completed by 1867. The Great Western Railway was never far from the action. It was instrumental in ensuring that four nominally independent companies were each responsible for one of the stages in a line from Ruabon to Llangollen, Llangollen to Corwen, Corwen to Bala, and Bala to Dolgellau. The line became open throughout in 1868 and, with completion of the link from Dolgellau to the Cambrian at Barmouth Junction, within a year through-running across the whole of Wales became possible for the Great Western Railway, which was responsible for operating all the traffic on the line. Within this period a line had opened from Bangor down to Afon Wen where it was soon connected to the Cambrian's line to Pwllheli. Another line linked

This locomotive was rebuilt by the Tredegar Iron and Coal Company in 1905 and ran on the Trefil Tramroad. The joint use of flangeless wheels and steam locomotives in this country was a rare event indeed. (British Rail)

Corwen on the Ruabon – Dolgellau line with Ruthin, Denbigh and Mold in 1864, and yet another line connected Llandudno Junction with Bettws-y-Coed in 1867. Thus within the space of a decade, 1859 – 69, the whole railway complexion of Mid and North Wales had been completely transformed. This network might almost be described as dense in relation to the population that it served, and the whole area could now be regarded as being well-endowed in a railway sense.

One aspect makes a stark contrast between North and South Wales. In the South, the Great Western Railway had a permanent fight on its hands with the many other independent railways right up to the grouping in 1922. The London & North Western Railway in North Wales sooner or later amalgamated with, or purchased, the branch lines which adjoined it and had a comparatively straight-forward and untroubled existence.

One further line in North Wales merits inclusion, not because of its length (initially it was only 10 miles long), but because right up until nationalisation in 1948 it remained an anomaly. This was the **Wrexham, Mold & Connah's Quay**,

which did not go to Mold, but ran from Wrexham to Buckley and thence over the **Buckley Railway** to Connah's Quay. The line opened in 1866 and was primarily a mineral line. Despite serving a heavily industrialised area, it was always in competition with the Great Western Railway, and its finances never prospered. The line became a very desirable property in the eyes of Edward Watkin, Chairman of the Manchester, Sheffield & Lincoln Railway, which viewed it from Chester. This company, having in the meantime become the Great Central Railway, bided its time. It finally pounced to acquire the Wrexham line in 1897. So, when the grouping took place, this resulted in the apparently anomalous presence of the London & North Eastern Railway in Wales, which continued until nationalisation.

Narrow-gauge railways in Wales are very much a part of contemporary railway activity, but this is a very recent development for the **Festiniog** (1836), **Corris** (1859), **Glyn Valley** (1873), and **Talyllyn** (1865) **Railways** were all built primarily to carry slate from a quarry to a trans-shipment point, the first three to water-borne transport, and

A consignment from the Welsh Whisky Works at Frongoch, near Bala, receives close attention from the various interested parties.
(Gwynedd Archives Service)

the Talyllyn to the Aberystwyth and Welsh Coast Railway at Tywyn. All these lines subsequently developed their passenger traffic on the basis of a sound goods traffic whereas the **North Wales Narrow Gauge Railway**, which followed soon after in 1877, had no such foundation and soon ran into severe financial difficulties. As with the standard-gauge system, so also was much of the narrow-gauge system built during, or close to, the period under review. The importance of these narrow-gauge railways lay in their value to the local slate industry and, as that industry declined, so also did their own fortunes. Last-minute rescue from oblivion for the Festiniog and Talyllyn Railways in the post-war era by volunteer workers heralded, in fact, the upsurge of interest in railway preservation as we know it today.

Moving on from this frantic decade of construction it is apparent that, apart from the Cambrian Railways in the centre and the local, one main-line railways, the London & North Western and Great Western Railways had partitioned up the rest of Wales between them. There was one other major English company which was casting

envious eyes on the South Wales coalfield. This was the **Midland Railway**. The Midland had access to Hereford from which the obvious destination in South Wales was Swansea. By playing a calmly waiting game it achieved this objective with three adroit manoeuvres and remarkably little capital expenditure. But it must be noted that the three companies concerned all had major problems. The first stage was an offer in 1869 to work the **Hereford, Hay & Brecon Railway** which had running powers over the Brecon & Merthyr into Brecon. Five years later the Midland leased the **Swansea Vale Railway** and, shortly afterwards, agreed to work the **Neath & Brecon Railway** from Brecon down to a junction with the **Swansea Vale**, thus completing the link between Hereford and Swansea. The Midland Railway made full use of its powers by running through passenger services from Swansea to Birmingham. But the line never generated the traffic which the Midland had in mind when it first cast its eyes over the Border.

As part of the improved service to Ireland through Fishguard, the G.W.R. constructed a heavily engineered line around Swansea. This photograph, (left) taken around 1909, contrasts with the almost simultaneous construction of a river bridge for the Lampeter, Aberayron and New Quay Light Railway (above).
(British Rail, National Library of Wales)

In 1889 the Maenclochog Railway in Pembrokeshire was put up for sale by auction. The importance of Fishguard was clearly appreciated but it was left to the G.W.R. to realise it. (National Library of Wales)

A Taff Vale Railway brake van with the guard, Richard Jones of Cathays Depot, on the right. In the centre is the shunter with his lamp and pole, c. 1900. (Miss B. Jones)

The G.W.R. went to considerable lengths to publicise the opening of its new route to Ireland through Fishguard in 1906, such as the advertisements on this bus in London. (British Rail)

At the turn of the century many companies introduced steam rail-motors to make branch line traffic more economic. This example was operated by the L.N.W.R. on the Prestatyn-Dyserth branch.
(Clwyd Record Office)

The military traffic at Trawsfynydd was such that the G.W.R. had, in effect, a second station to deal with special troop movements.
(Casgliad Angharad ac Arwel Gwynedd Roberts)

Corris conversation piece:- locomotive No. 2 at Corris Station on 23rd May 1914. (D.S. George)

Courtship and Competition

In South Wales the rest of the 1870s and early 1880s saw railway traffic increasing overall and with it an increase in congestion on the railways and in the docks. Naturally, such congestion did not please the coal-owners, who were also unhappy at the monopolies exercised by the Taff Vale and Rhymney Railways in the Cardiff area. A groundswell of unrest consequently built up among the coal-owners. Spearheaded by the redoubtable David Davies of the Ocean Coal Company, this culminated in the construction of a brand new system. This was the **Barry Dock & Railway Company**, a classic example of an integrated transport system. The docks and railway were superbly laid out and engineered, the railway of necessity because all the obvious and easiest routes to the hinterland were already occupied by other railways. As originally opened in 1889 the Barry Railway could not have had a simpler structure. A single main line ran from Barry to Pontypridd, and on to Trehafod in the Rhondda Valley, a distance of less than twenty miles. Traffic prospered, and therefore, to some extent, reduced the Taff Vale's profits. This ensured a fair degree of enmity between the two companies, and the Barry accordingly built a branch to the Rhymney Valley in 1901. Because this branch cut right across the Taff and Rhymney Valleys, it needed engineering works on a massive scale, including two spectacular viaducts at Llanbradach and Taffs Well. With the completion of this branch it may be said that major railway construction in Wales had ended.

But the construction of the Barry main line and its branch should not obscure the fact that, concurrently, two more railways were being built inland from Port Talbot. The Afan Valley above Port Talbot had possessed a railway for some years, the **South Wales Mineral Railway** of 1863, which had started life as one of Brunel's broad-gauge creations solely to serve a colliery. On the conversion of the South Wales Railway to standard-gauge, it had nearly closed. A more strategic use of the Afan Valley was as a route for conveying coal from the top of the Rhondda Valley, entered via a tunnel, to the ports of West Glamorgan. This was the philosophy behind the creation of the **Rhondda & Swansea Bay Railway** which, in 1894, finally reached Swansea, where much of the support for the railway lay.

This line was followed four years later by the **Port Talbot Railway** which sought and provided an alternative outlet to Porthcawl for the coal from the Llynfi and Garw valleys. The Great Western Railway successfully wooed the three lines in this area and had effectively obtained control of them all by 1908.

This courtship of the Rhondda & Swansea Bay Railway was somewhat disingenuous, for the Great Western Railway had an ulterior motive in acquiring the company. At the turn of the century it had embarked on a massive scheme to construct a new harbour at Fishguard, primarily to improve the Irish traffic, but also with the possibility of tapping off passenger and mail traffic from the transatlantic liners as they made their way up to Liverpool. Ideally, to capitalise on this potential new traffic required that the fierce gradients on either side of the approaches to Swansea should be bypassed. The Rhondda & Swansea Bay Company's river swing-bridge at Neath would greatly facilitate construction of the by-pass, known as the Swansea District Lines, and hence, once control of the company had been obtained in 1906, the bridge was duly incorporated. Sadly, the tremendous publicity which accompanied the visit of the liner 'Mauretania' to Fishguard in 1909 was an ephemeral event. The advent of World War 1, and the displacement of Liverpool by Southampton, spelt the end of the Great Western Railway's commendable commercial enterprise.

Although almost peripheral to this account, the Great Western had radically improved the service from London and the West Country some years previously by constructing the Severn Tunnel. Opened in 1886 after taking twelve years to complete, it was one of the great engineering feats of the last century. But, by its very nature, it is not capable of making such a dramatic visual impact as, say, the present Severn road bridge. But the tunnel eliminated the long haul around

Before road motor transport became established, livestock was normally moved by train, such as this scene at Lampeter on the occasion of the Horse Fair, c. 1905. (British Rail)

Gloucester and, as much as anything, was used by the coal trains coming from the Aberdare-Pontypool line.

In the early 1890s the internal combustion engine had not yet been recognised as a future means of road transport and a deadly competitor of the railways. So Parliament passed legislation to encourage the construction of light railways, which were subject to less stringent conditions than normal railways, as a means of improving communications beteeen small communities which did not already possess a railway. The concept was very successful in France. But, in this country, relatively little mileage was constructed under these provisions. The standard-gauge lines built as light railways included the **Tanat Valley Light Railway** opened in 1904, and the **Lampeter, Aberayron & New Quay Light**

Apart from the bustle of activity at Newtown Goods Yard, Cardiff, the presence of both pre- and post-grouping railway companies' wagons will be noted.
(British Rail)

Railway, which never reached New Quay, and opened in 1911. The **Burry Port & Gwendraeth Valley Railway** also took advantage of the Act to legalise its operations. This railway had operated officially since its beginning in 1868 as a mineral line but, unofficially, had also carried passengers, using devious means to charge fares. In 1909 it was reconstructed as a light railway and thereafter carried its passengers officially. Authorisation was also given for other light railways, including one between Llandeilo and Lampeter, and one from Swansea to Port Eynon in Gower. But neither was ever constructed. Although the narrow-gauge railways do not form a central part of this account, it might be noted that both the **Welshpool & Llanfair** and the **Vale of Rheidol Railways** were authorised under the Light Railways Act.

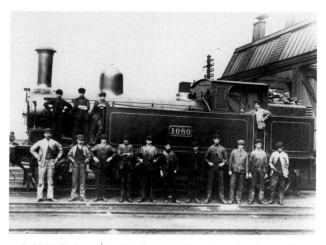

L.N.W.R. locomotive No. 1080 at Saltney Ferry Junction, with a number of the shed staff. (Clwyd Record Office)

A.L.N.W.R. Coal tank locomotive at Pattison's Crossing near Brymbo. (Clwyd Record Office)

A Carmarthen-bound train at Llandeilo, with an unusual double-heading by L.N.W.R. and G.W.R. locomotives. (National Museum of Wales)

Aberystwyth Station was rebuilt by the G.W.R. in 1926 and this photograph was probably taken soon afterwards. (National Library of Wales)

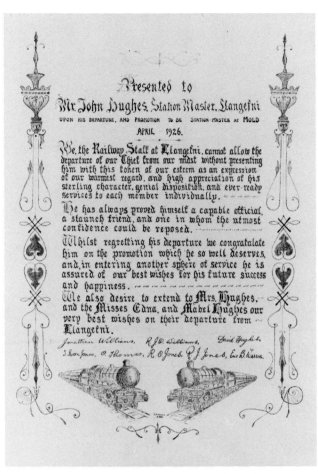

This illuminated address was presented to John Hughes, Station Master of Llangefni, on his promotion to a similar post at Mold. Although Llangefni was in the heart of L.M.S. territory the locomotives would suggest that the artist was influenced by another company. (Mrs. E. Leadbeater)

Private owner wagons considerably enlivened the Welsh railway scene and these examples give some idea of the variety that was to be encountered. The earliest wagons had dumb buffers at both ends but the friable nature of Welsh coal soon made it necessary to have sprung buffers on at least one end of the vehicle, as seen here on the Ocean wagon. (British Rail)

One of the ubiquitous G.W.R. saddle-tank locomotives No. 1638 hauls a train of assorted private owner wagons near the clay pits at Tondu. The centre wagon is of the early short-wheelbase dumb-buffered type. (British Rail)

No. 1547, a Webb four-cylinder compound locomotive, at Saltney Ferry Junction Depot, c. 1928. (C. A. J. Nevett Collection)

A contractor's train carrying workmen to the construction site of the Ystrad Fellte Waterworks, near Hirwaun

American locomotives being serviced at Ebbw Junction Depot, Newport, in 1944, preparatory to working in Britain and, shortly afterwards, in France following the Normandy landings. (U.S. Government)

Locomotive No. 2625, of a type introduced by the G.W.R. to work the coal traffic on the Aberdare – Pontypool line, was used in World War 2 for target practice in North Pembrokeshire by aircraft. It was whitewashed to assist the aircrew but, nevertheless, survived to continue working after the War. (British Rail)

Many features of the Snowdon Mountain Railway are unique to the railways of Britain, not least the rapid transition from the peaceful shores of Llyn Padarn to the jagged beauty of the summits of Snowdonia. (Glyn Davies)

One of the more enchanting aspects of the industrial railway scene must be this portrayal of 'Britomart' pulling a train load of waste material at the Pen-yr-Orsedd Slate Quarry in 1952. (J.I.C. Boyd)

Both locomotive No. 3586 and its coach have the air of a long-departed era but this photograph was taken at Cowbridge in 1947. (Ian L. Wright)

Merthyr High Street Station in August 1951 was a hive of activity. Brunel's original train shed can be seen in the left background. (Ian L. Wright)

The Swansea – Pontarddulais auto-train at Swansea Victoria Station in 1949, headed by Webb Coal Tank 27625 which still carries its pre-nationalisation livery. (Ian L. Wright)

Zenith and Slow Decline

During the years around the turn of the century, the fortunes of the Taff Vale and Rhymney Railways were riding high while those of the Bute Docks Company were of a mediocre nature. This led to various proposals for amalgamation. The only tangible outcome was a change of name for the latter to the **Cardiff Railway Company**, and to construction of the last coal-oriented railway in Wales. The intention was to carry coal to the company's docks as well as handling it within the docks. The line which the company constructed, at very considerable expense, for it was only seven miles long, ran from a junction with the Rhymney Railway on the edge of Cardiff to a junction with the Taff Vale at Treforest. It thus involved collaboration with both these companies. The Taff Vale would have none of this and, after the inaugural coal-train in 1909, promptly closed the junction which never reopened, despite prolific litigation. In a sense this represented the climax of competition between the coal-carrying railways for, although this litigation carried on during World War 1, reason finally prevailed. In 1917 the General Manager of the Rhymney Railway assumed the same position with the Taff Vale and Cardiff Railways, and collaboration proceeded from then until the grouping.

The year 1913 saw the zenith of the coal trade in South Wales and a flourishing traffic in tourists in North Wales. With the outbreak of war in the following year the tourist trade naturally suffered. But coal traffic barely faltered despite having its direction of travel reversed. Instead of flowing downhill to the ports, the export trade was greatly reduced and much of the coal was sent northwards, particularly to the Grand Fleet in Scapa Flow. (At the outbreak of World War I, the Royal Navy's battlefleets, like those of other navies, were coal-fired; it was the new oil-fired warships, built during the war, that pointed to the future decline of the Welsh coal markets for maritime use.) Gargantuan quantities of coal were moved, some over the Brecon & Merthyr's mountainous line but, at the end of the war, the collapse of world markets,

changed patterns of trade and the exhausted, run-down condition of the railways made radical changes inevitable.

These altered economic conditions had already been anticipated by the government and, the concept of nationalisation being rejected, the outcome was a grouping of all the independent railways into four large companies between 1921 and 1923. In Wales this meant that the London & North Western and Midland Railway routes and those companies over which they exerted a controlling influence passed smoothly into the London, Midland & Scottish Railway. The erstwhile Wrexham, Mold & Connah's Quay Railway became part of the London & North Eastern Railway and so provided that company with a very useful entry into north-east Wales. The remaining companies in Wales became part of the Great Western Railway. The Barry, Cambrian, Taff Vale, Rhymney and Alexandra (Newport) Railways became constituent companies, while all the other lesser companies became subsidiaries. By this subtle distinction, honour and prestige were satisfied, but the pre-grouping Great Western Railway was, nevertheless, the completely dominant influence. It slowly standardised many operating and organisational practices, including the re-building of many of the locomotives which it had acquired. Given the dense network of competing lines in South Wales which passed to the Great Western, it is not surprising that there were about 70 miles of duplicated route. One might have anticipated that, with the decline in the coal trade in the 1920s, this duplication would have been rapidly eliminated. But such rationalisation took place only on a very small scale, albeit with the demolition of the Llanbradach Viaduct and the closure of the Taff Vale's Locomotive Works in Cardiff. The London, Midland & Scottish Railway had no such duplication with its much sparser network, and rationalisation as a result of grouping did not occur.

These comments should not obscure the changes which did take place as a result of declining traffic in the 1920s and which tend to be overshadowed by more recent memories of the

This scene could well be regarded as portraying the archetypal branch-line train, in this instance it is the Monmouth – Severn Tunnel Junction train approaching Brockwear Halt in the Wye Valley in March 1958. (R.O. Tuck)

post-Beeching era. This decline was due both to economic factors and to the sharp increase in road transport. Indeed, the Cambrian had introduced a motor-bus service from Pwllheli to Nevin as early as 1906 rather than extend its line, and it is easy to forget that in the period 1930 – 33 services over twenty passenger lines throughout Wales were withdrawn. Many of them minor lines but, nevertheless, it is an indication that the railway system had passed its zenith. Yet despite this contraction, the railways actively promoted tourism and holiday traffic (although it remained for the Beeching Report to reveal how uneconomic much of the high season traffic really was). Indeed, even in 1853, the prospectus of the proposed North & South Wales Railway waxed eloquent on the thousands of tourists who would be able to enjoy the scenic beauties of Wales when the line was built. Shortly afterwards the Aberystwyth & Welsh Coast Railway became actively involved in the hotel business, seeing tourism as an essential element of its revenue. (At Aberystwyth the railway hotel, designed in baronial splendour by J. P. Seddon, became the first building to house the newly-established University of Wales (1872).) Later in the century the spa towns of Mid-Wales, the resort towns of the North Wales coast and the Cambrian Coast, and Tenby, served by the **Pembroke and Tenby Railway**, all prospered by virtue of the railborne tourist, while Llangollen early on benefited from the day-excursionists from Manchester and Merseyside. In the 1920s and 1930s the Great Western Railway, especially, promoted tourism, opening a number of additional halts on the Ruabon – Dolgellau line and developing Barry Island.

All this traffic faded away almost overnight when World War II started. Railway operation, now under central government control, became far more stringent than in the previous war. Again the railways moved prodigious quantities of men and materials not only on the main lines but on quiet branches where the location of training camps, depots, and other military establishments saw more traffic through some country stations than they had seen in the whole of their existence. The end of the

Cefn Viaduct, on the Brecon and Merthyr line between Merthyr and Morlais Junction, saw its last service in 1961 but still stands imposingly today. (Glyn Davies)

The end draws nigh as the last ex-L.N.W.R. locomotive in Wales, No. 49064, complete with snow-plough which would only fit this type of locomotive, prepares to leave Tredegar Shed for the breaker's yard in August 1959. All the staff in the photograph had started their careers with the L.M.S. (R.O. Tuck)

One of the infrequent goods trains on the Brecon – Builth Road line passes Aberedw. The low height of the platform required the use of portable steps for passenger trains. (Glyn Davies)

war saw the railways exhausted, deprived of investment and suffering from a multitude of other problems. This time nationalisation was inevitable and in 1948, the London, Midland and Scottish and Great Western lines became the London Midland and Western Regions respectively of British Rail, but with some transfers for boundary convenience.

One feature which had a certain visual appeal and added variety to the railway scene also disappeared at this time, but this arose from the nationalisation of the coal industry rather than the railways. This was the private owner wagon. Whereas in most other parts of the country minerals were carried in the railway companies' wagons, in Wales this was not the case, and they were largely carried in wagons belonging to the colliery, factor or shipping agent. These wagons bore a great variety of liveries and markings due to the need in the mid-nineteenth century for a

distinctive marking which could be easily recognised by those in the docks and marshalling sidings who could not read. These markings developed until many of them became outright travelling advertisements for their owners' products. Even when carrying solely the name of the company, such as Ocean, Marine, Naval, Maritime or Navigation, the purpose and destination of the product was patently obvious and certainly evocative.

Following nationalisation, despite rapidly deteriorating finances, the railway system in Wales continued relatively unchanged for some six years. But in the decade from 1955 to 1965, a series of closures left whole areas of Wales devoid of any rail connection. This reduction in route mileage was so dramatic that it was almost the reverse of the great expansion a century earlier. While the lover of railways frequently rues the disappearance of the railways from so much of the landscape it must also

A rare line-up of express locomotives at Pengam Sidings, Cardiff, in March 1961, waiting to haul their excursion trains back to West Wales after a rugby international. This was the last occasion on which all-steam working took place. (R.O. Tuck)

be remembered that, had the internal combustion engine arrived thirty years earlier, most of these lines would never have been built in the first place. Since 1965 there have been few closures. The network appears to have stabilised, with an operating philosophy today based largely on high-speed passenger travel and the bulk movement of freight.

Within this short account it has clearly only been possible to cover the standard gauge railway history of Wales in the most superficial manner. Nothing has been said of the changes in locomotives and rolling stock which, to many people, are the only interesting aspects of railways. Nor has anything been said of the human and social dramas which are inseparable from any evolving system; the long hours, low pay and tyrannical discipline which the men endured and their struggle for humane treatment and trade union recognition; the characters in the history,

such as Cornelius Lundie of the Rhymney, Ammon Beasley of the Taff Vale, David Davies of the Cambrian and Barry Railways or John Ceiriog Hughes (1832 – 1887) the most popular Welsh poet of his day who wrote much of his verse while he was General Manager of the Van Railway in Mid-Wales. Apparently, he never once in his poetry made the slightest reference to railways of any kind, although the hours of inactivity on that railway greatly exceeded the other kind! Each of these aspects could fill a book by themselves and sadly could not be pursued here. Many of them have in fact been so treated in full-length books and to these the reader is heartily commended. There he may learn, in far greater depth, of the panoply of events which constitute the ever-changing history of the railways of Wales.

Being prepared for duty-locomotive No. 7023 'Penrice Castle' at Canton Depot, Cardiff, in December 1956. (R.O. Tuck)

Exchanging the token for single-line working on the Central Wales line through the Sugar Loaf Tunnel with a Shrewsbury – Swansea (Victoria) train in 1952. (R.O. Tuck)

The coast line of the Cambrian Railways was not one on which high speeds pertained for reasons which this view along the Dyfi Estuary makes patently clear. It was originally planned to cross the Dyfi near this point with a viaduct similar to the one at Barmouth but the strong tides and deep sand on the Ynyslas side forced the abandonment of this project. (Glyn Davies)

The End of the Line (1) – literally as well as metaphorically, as the G.W.R. – R.R. Joint Line viaduct at Quakers Yard is demolished in 1969. The viaduct had suffered from the effects of mining subsidence as the timber supports make clear. (British Rail)

The End of the Line (2) – the last passenger to leave Aberdare High Level Station in 1964 with the closure of the Neath – Pontypool Road line.
(Glyn Davies)

The End of the Line (3) – in this case the end of the famous Star Class is nigh, as No. 4056 'Princess Margaret'' prepares to leave Cardiff Station on 29th July 1955. (R.O. Tuck)

British Rail's bulk freight operations are typified in this view of iron ore being moved in 100 tonne wagons from Port Talbot to Llanwern Steel Works and passing a bulk chemical train on its way to Baglan Bay.
(British Rail)

One of British Rail's Inter-City 125 trains at Newport. These trains provide a high-speed passenger service between South Wales and London.
(British Rail)

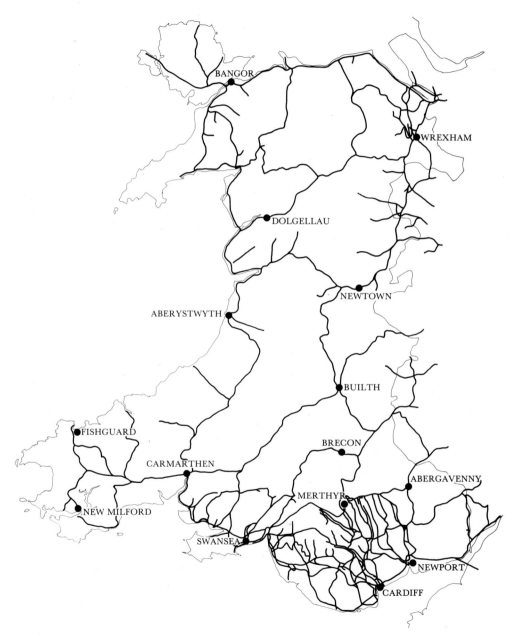

This map shows the railway network of Wales in 1920, by which time the network had attained its maximum extent. (Some very short branches have been omitted for reasons of clarity).